Absence of Clouds

Also by Thérèse Corfiatis and published by Ginninderra Press

Seasons of the Soul (with Anne Landers)
Emissaries of Light
Northern Lights
The Edge of Tranquillity
The Boy Who Loved the Moon
Handfuls of Promise
Moonlight Wine (Pocket Poets)
A Thousand Birds Were Singing (Picaro Poets)
House of Dreams

Thérèse Corfiatis

Absence of Clouds

For Hazel

Absence of Clouds
ISBN 978 1 76041 393 4
Copyright © text Thérèse Corfiatis 2017
Cover from an original painting by Beverley Ravanelli

First published 2017 by
Ginninderra Press
PO Box 3461 Port Adelaide 5015 Australia
www.ginninderrapress.com.au

Contents

Absence of Clouds	7
Early Autumn Rains	8
Autumn Trees and Birds	9
Beacons	10
Black Cockatoos	11
Blessings	12
Cloud Haiku	13
Contented Cows	14
Dominions	15
Dove Lake	16
Drive to Preston	17
Evening Journey	18
From the Pier at Night	19
Haiku	20
If There Were a Thousand Moons	21
Invaders of Ulverstone	22
Last Day of Summer	23
Pillared Flanks of Green	24
River of Glass	25
Soul Food at Picnic Point	26
Spaces and Moments	28
Spring's Bounty	29
The Speech of Trees	30
The Window	31
Winter Storm Front	32
Reflections in Time	33
Relationship of Geology to People	34
Word Catcher	35
Longing	36
All Saint's Day	37

Books Find a New Home	38
Nine Thirty-five	39
Landscape of Kindness	40
My Beloved	41
Thoughts on Autism	42
Visit to my Birthplace	43
After the Fall	44
No More the Silent Tread	45
Assimilation of the Map Makers	46
Return of the Map Makers	48
Indigenous Veterans of Two World Wars	49
Tree-sitter of the Tarkine	50
Goodness	52
A Dog's Tale	54
The Itinerant	56
Reflections on Budapest	58
The Bridge at Csikrákos	61
Towards Istanbul	64
Aghios Nikolaos	66
Flight over Arabian Peninsula	69

Absence of Clouds

blue sky grieves
an absence of clouds

the blue is vast
it dazzles cruelly
sky's fabric stretched
into a dome-shaped drum

birds sing and fly
voyaging the drum's oscillations
high views
of earth's curving horizons
unobstructed
feathered pumping wings
embracing the planet
as a body embraces a heart

Early Autumn Rains

I stand in autumn rain
trees transformed by water
into breathing, shimmering spirits

Cool spears of wetness
bathe my face
bare arms shine like oil

Droplets slide
like transparent blood
from my fingers to the earth

Infused with eucalyptus scent
both trees and I
stand cleansed and strong

Autumn Trees and Birds

What are all these surging shoals
amber-russet rustlings, all shook out
these descending notes of birdsong?

A segue of movement, colour, light
leaf-fall and melody
rolling into the ear, the heart, the soul

This small moment of perfection
memory enough
to endure, from one autumn to another

Beacons

Bordering the path
small white daisies
unfold to morning's light

tiny beacons
track the sun's course
until evening shadows fall

flowers close
in mathematical precision
a silent infolding

yellow hearts petalled over
suspended in sleep
awaiting the sun's roll call

Black Cockatoos

They flew low
so close to my head
this black, glossy pair
yellow-flecked tails flashing
like airborne sunflowers

that the beat of feathered wings
fanned my hair
as I looked up, laughing
rejoicing in their shrieks
revelling in their freedom

Blessings

Clouds are moving meditations
mantras murmured in the sky
pouring breath into the ocean
blessings for the watcher's eye

River seems unearthly still
silken panels undulate
reflecting images of birds and trees
blessings sent for those who wait

Cloud Haiku

white clouds skittering
prayer flags across the sky
entreaty heaven

Contented Cows

cows laying down on the job
green coverlets
soft under bone
munching merrily

a herd of sun-warmed backs

Dominions

castellation of cloud
blue-grey dominions
cling low to hills –
a walled medieval city

Dove Lake

Tasmanian Highlands

In silence by the lake
each to our own thoughts –
enraptured by shifting waters
the mountain's curving cradle,
spaces fresh with scent and colour
rock, earth, trees and native flowers –
our eyes met
unspoken feelings
laid down deep, like the lake.

All this and more
we knew
and carried
like an ancient weathered stone
held in our hands
indestructible
a thing of permanence –
standing in silence
together by the lake.

Drive to Preston

North-west Tasmania

A fragrant drive inland
flanked by eucalyptus and pine
tunnels of wind and greenness
panoramas of far-off mountains
deep-cut valleys

climbing higher, away from ocean
stone and ancient memories
of a people long gone
a residue of their existence
in restless treetops
lingering like warm sunlight
laying soft hands upon my head

Who breathes against my cheek?
Who beckons from the dappled shadows?

A raven lifts up and turns to meet my eye
blood upon his beak.

Evening Journey

crescent moon
a unicorn's horn
silver, frozen

tufted clouds lift and splay
a mane parted
by atmospheric winds

soft stirrings
a gentle gallop
through jewelled stars

heaven's mighty head
harnessed
by night's starry rein

a dream run
on an evening journey
towards home

From the Pier at Night

Ulverstone

Wind-bustled up the estuary
gulls fly in mobs
settling on green river banks
a coverlet of moving feathers

An immense sky lifts up
Dial Ranges outlined in sunset's dimming light
transforming from fiery red to deepest pink,
lush apricot with hints of peach –
all gone now
except in memory upon the page

Water laps it tongues
around the bridge's pylons
cars traversing east and west
headlights gleam like cat's eyes

A solitary fisherman drops a line
gazing out towards the ocean's roar
moonlit benedictions anoint his head
both he and I, lost in contemplations
apart, but connected to our time and space

Are fragile earthbound thoughts
enough to drive the cosmos
beyond eternity?

Haiku

dandelion spume
windswept white puffs drift on air
points of reference

If There Were a Thousand Moons

If there were a thousand moons
like the one I see tonight
my eyes would never waver
never look downwards again

I would spend my whole life
staring upwards
hypnotised by beauty
held captive to this saffron light

to sublime heavens
where stars pulse like tiny hearts
drawing me into other worlds
never wanting to return

I could learn to be a mountain
to stand for eternity beneath the sky
if there were a thousand moons
like the one I see tonight

Invaders of Ulverstone

North-west Tasmania

thunder rolls across rooftops
like a marching army

cymbals smash
windows shaken, vibrating

lightning hurls electrical jagged arms
huge tentacles clutch heavy dark clouds

silver slices the sky apart
a bevy of flashing metal swords

Thor's roar echoes across hills
fading away into the night

a gradual settling down
Valhalla's hall has shut its door

Last Day of Summer

The last day of summer
swelled in a blue triumph
pressing out against horizons
pushing down upon a cobalt-blue sea

Light composed of purest beauty
assaults the eye
like glints off a warrior's shield
a force so immense
it built into legions
marching across treetops and hills
demanding songs from the throats of birds
spreading scent from green herb beds
compelling bees to hum far into dusk

Beyond the black tents of peaked hills
the last day of summer
shot out its quivering arrows
fingers now stilled, bows lowered
settling to rest
awaiting the advent of a million lustrous stars
the earth in liege
to all that lives and breathes
its many gods of shape and form and colour
replete at last.

Pillared Flanks of Green

It is the space between the trees
between the pillared flanks of green
that draws me in
an archway to another dimension

I want to hover there
suspended in greyness
feeling rain, moonlight
rising sun
wind shifting about me
like another layer of skin

Let me melt into the greyness
this way and that
a feather drifting
lighter than a dream

River of Glass

I come to the river
kneel, dip my hands
cold honeyed water
silken-soft to the touch

My body stoops
this flesh-covered skeleton
veins, muscle, ligament
holds all of my being

We mirror each other
water-bound entities
this river of glass
reflects clouds shaped like bone

Light shines above us
darkness below us
between these two places
only river, and me

Soul Food at Picnic Point

West Ulverstone

Chaotic winter shoreline –
tortured tree trunks
driftwood, kelp and seaweed
lay strewn across the beach
as if the sea
brewed up a noisy carnival
and left its scattered flotsam
tin cans, plastic cups –
evidence of night's stormy revelry.

Heavy-lidded foam
rolls in the surf
midday's cappuccino,
eyes feasting on a froth-rich sea.

Ocean drums like running feet
towards a rendezvous,
soft dunes and scrub
heaped high with shells and pebbles
skeletons of little crabs
like a platter
of left-over hors d'oeuvres.

Soul food at Picnic Point –
relief from the frenzy
of demanding days,
all this evaporates with lifting sea spray
carried off like crumbs
from a shook-out tablecloth
into the chill blue sky –
angst, dispersed to the light-filled air.

Spaces and Moments

Patches of blue-grey sky
hover between bare branches
dry leaves clack like castanets

Those rhythms pacify a nervous heart
like distant train wheels trundling
a multitude of clucking hens –
reassuring cadence

And then
a growing awareness
of pulses in the body
rise and fall of ribcage
the neck tapping signals
hidden in warm veins
the heart's secret codes
singing to an existence
larger than life itself
of a life without
of separated thought

of these two things becoming one

Spring's Bounty

North-west Tasmania

from a high vantage point
land falls away
peaks and troughs resemble a woman's body
adorned in patchwork fields of jasmine, mint, and emerald
tree branches reveal bedecked fingers, jewelled
with fruit, blossom and bud

all this she gives to us
beauty for eyes, nourishment for body
sun's warmth, a gift
rain's cool offering, a blessing

tread gently upon her form
for it is here many creatures walk
people, flocks of sheep, herds of cattle
birds, insects, reptiles, trout in the running river

let us protect, replenish her
for we are nurtured, amazed by all she does
by the subtle season's shifting quarters
their splendour and reward

let us honour her in all ways
keep clean her waters, forest and wild places
for her body, harbouring our home
continues to renew our needs

for it is here, in these green valleys
spring's bounty will always come

The Speech of Trees

a cradle's song
whoosh, whoosh, whoosh

wood creaks, limbs crack
bark flip-flaps-falls
helicopter-whirlings

gusted treetops
sway in unison
choirs surging on air

a voice like no other

the speech of trees

The Window

glass square

within its frame
a trapped landscape
grey sky, glaring
stippled-doughy cloud
metallic white light
highlighting edges

sky, in broken columns
sliced by cylindrical
trunks of trees
thrusting upwards
cut off
at the frame's edge

window, contained

Winter Storm Front

North-west Tasmania

Icy Antarctic blasts
sweep across the island
trees bent, an agony of twisted limbs
swirling leaves jettisoned on air
birds shriek out alarms
clawing, clinging to footholds

All melds into a frenzy
senses confused
colours, sounds, smells overlap

Ocean churns and froths
erupting against the sky
as horizontal rain slants in
whipping along streets
roofs clattering
a million cutting knives

Heavy clouds like dark grey sails
fill the sky
rudderless, surging forwards
an armada threatening
no quarter given in any direction

Reflections in Time

Birds swoop low over water
light uplifts a wave-tossed sea
clouds move, like troupes of dancers
if only they could be

Gums lean, bent down by sandy shores
an orchestra of trees
songs of rain and wind and storm
played out in swirling leaves

Yachts scud, like fluttering handkerchiefs
sails straining, full and fine
vanishing at far horizons,
reflections held in time

Relationship of Geology to People

melt-water
a steady trickle
builds in impetus
becomes a swifter flow
entering pristine lakes and rivers

glaciers gouge
scraping, scouring
U-shaped valleys formed
plunging into deep
water-laden chasms

mountains rise
gigantic rock and stony morass
carve out singular journeys
linking land to sea
skerries scattered, cast adrift

lava spills
relentless, unstoppable
expunging all in its path
bearer of entombment
life extinguished

people of every time and place
have lain down offerings
to mountains, stone and water
seeking benevolence
from nature's unforgiving power –
a force still shaping the existence
of all who walk this ever-changing earth

Word Catcher

thought glides
a hawk on silent wings
circling, watching

the mind
is like a field of grass
exposed to all

far below, words run
like tiny mice scattering
seeking shelter

Longing

Winter days shorten
weave a haunting melancholy.
Strange cries
drift in from the sea –
Is it wind
or the shriek of birds
so unsettling me?

A fractured, darkening sky
envelops all –
I feel splintered, as if
fragments of myself
are spearing outwards
into the cold night air.

In this altered state
I am caught between two spheres –
no middling place
no joy, no fear.

There is only longing –
all-encompassing
coursing like a river
to the sea.

All Saint's Day

quivering melting trees
shade the way
where – a road cutting through
green spirals
in another time and place,
women such as I
would have fallen
upon our knees
worshipping them

Books Find a New Home

Books sit heavy
not entirely in neat lines
some protrude outwards
others, inwards
like a Mexican wave
saying '*Hola*
welcome to your new home
we await the touch of your fingers'

I glance along bookcases
life's decades in their pages
like old friends
remaining steadfast and true

Nine Thirty-five

nine thirty-five
evening light still glimmers
long summer days
draw unending beauty to the eye

sky layers itself in colours
rising ever higher up
encrusted now, to reveal starry patterns
Orion's Belt, the Southern Cross
constellations formed long, long ago
billions of earthbound souls
still watch them far below

and a memory comes
slipping into mind like a drifting leaf
of a small girl
head laid upon her arms
propped against the window sill
eyes gazing heavenwards
thought running free

raptures flow into her
as if swimming through a mighty ocean –
fathomless wonder, immensity and splendour

decades later
nine thirty-five
another summer evening
holds her hostage to its sky
sitting there, unaware of time
no past, no present, no future

enthralling still

Landscape of Kindness

Kindness creates a foothold
its constancy, like stone, a comfort
its bulk and power offer solidity
showing familiar landscapes
for us to navigate
a sense of place
human warmth desired

Such is it, to know the contours
of a beloved one's face
held within our hands
feeling the ridges, dips, hollows and plumpness
of brows, eyes, cheeks and lips
a map constructed for us
revealing a way to tenderness, to love

My Beloved

banish my illusions
leave only what is real –
the eyes of my sons, shining with light
the touch of their father's hand
voices and faces of those I love
the living memory of those long gone

reveal your beauty
manifest your wonders –
jewelled wings of birds
a copper moon veiled behind burnished clouds
ocean's song, wind's keening
ever-present rise and set of sun
breathing green forests
rain falling like a song

I am less than a particle of light –
all that you are, all that you know
surpasses my understanding
draw me, my beloved
like a flame leaping into the air
into a billion scattered stars
devotees all, dancing in eternal darkness

look upon me with benevolence
this tiny life a mere nanosecond –
so that when it ends
each fragment may be returned to the whole

Thoughts on Autism

My firstborn possesses
a changeling's purity of spirit –
creativity and beauty
pour from his fertile mind

In bygone centuries
his strangeness, his need for ritual
would have been stepped upon
crushed underfoot

Mothers know the power of love
fight for what is just and right
will go screaming into the night
in order to see fairness thrive

For what else
do humans live
if not to serve and care
and freely give?

My words are a voice
for those who cannot speak
for those who feel dispossession and pain
and live it each day, again and again

My words are a voice for those never heard
for those who can never 'be'
for a mountain of souls
to rise up on strong wings and fly free

Visit to my Birthplace

Hobart

A monolith, Mt Wellington loomed
resurrecting decades of memories
returning my grandparents to me
my little brothers and sisters
my mother's smile,
as snow glinted in winter sun.

The beauty of cloud-shadows
moving across the mountain
like rippling fabric on the wind,
the intensity of stone
neither blue nor purple
but something in between,
fills my heart.

Houses tumble down hills
like children's toys
spilling into the valley,
boats rocking on the river Derwent
in folds as soft as crumpled silk,
pale-gold sandstone buildings
line Macquarie Street's green-cloaked avenue of oak
the toll of St David's Cathedral bell.

It caused tears to brim
my very breath gasped in.
I wanted to swallow those memories
into myself,
grow fat on them.

After the Fall

I arrived to find my brother
sitting outdoors with our mother
recuperating from her recent fall

Autumn sunlight emphasised bruises –
a yellow-purple stain
slips down from blackened, puffy eyes
washing over each cheek
spreading lower on her neck
like an ebb-tide mark
against a fleshy bank of ligament and bone

On her left forehead
a bulging mound
stitched tight in black thread
like a smooth, stuffed aubergine
legacy of the forward fall

Watching every move
I follow her into the house
as she tilts forwards, bent at the waist
a jerky shuffling gait –
the forward fall, not good at all

To know her this way
has altered the memory of how she was before

I love her even more

No More the Silent Tread

No more the silent tread
touch of silken fur
A paw raised upwards to my face
green eyes I so adored

No more the bite, done gently though
to quell the hand; enough!
His stripes and whirls; black, copper, cream
a living work of art

No more the sound of purring
his heart upon my breast
His playful dash up branch and tree
the flopping down to rest

No more watching starlit skies
in the front room of our house
Upon his blanket, safe and warm
stock still, quiet as a mouse

No more his cry, in reply to mine
the inquiring, curious face
No more the sharing of our days
just an empty aching space

Assimilation of the Map Makers

for the First Australians

Taken from tribal lands
the adults went to missions and stations
and children into Christian classrooms.
They learnt about the Holy Spirit
and a man who was nailed to a cross.
This probably frightened them in the beginning.

They were given tobacco, flour, sugar and tea
in lieu of salary –
it made them sick, life-spans shortened.
The children learnt to sing 'God Save the King' –
unbeknown to their teachers
they already possessed timeless songs of their own.

Songs were streamlined to the land –
each outcrop, waterhole, river, salt pan
sand dune, mountain range, tree –
Millions of connection points,
a map of every black footprint
that ever walked the land,
a musical reference
passed down in memory banks of song –
It is a mystery older than Stonehenge
older than the builders of the Aztec pyramids,
more complex than a Bach concerto.

They were the original map makers of this land.

They sang to an existence
of their Ancestors' dreaming,
walking country into perpetual being,
returning, when death became imminent
to the source of conception
joining the Ancestors who had walked before them
life's circle complete.

Return of the Map Makers

There is a stand of old gums
near my home.
Sometimes I think I see the ancient ones
watching the river run towards sea
silver hair lit up by the moon
footsteps crunching as they walk
singing country into being
or is it just fleeting shapes in the darkness
trees moving in the wind?

Indigenous Veterans of Two World Wars

Fighting on distant shores
not just for our country
but in the hope
of attaining recognition and equality
profound sacrifices were laid down.

Proud families
sons and daughters
welcomed veterans home.
White Australians deemed it a non-event
a cruel version of their history.

No acknowledgement came.
Memory slipped back into sand
like a mirage in the desert.

Decades later
awareness came, like longed for rain
red poppies fed by blood and sweat
pinned to their chests in gratitude
marching together
side by side –
Australians, all, walking free.

Tree-sitter of the Styx Valley

Protector of forests
she sat precariously
on an elevated perch
month after month,
her only companions
singing birds, scudding clouds –
rain driving hard
pelting her temporary home
unable to dampen belief.

Far below
an army of followers
publicity organised
meals cooked in makeshift mess tents
road blocks set up
protestors fanning out
bodies on the front line.

High above, she looked out
on a place of great beauty
immovable, resolute
keeping warm, keeping positive
pondering the agony of a forest
stripped bare of its trees.

A fire forced her down
but in a newspaper story
recounting her vigil
she is smiling, looking happy
knowing part of the forest
is World Heritage listed,
untouched, left pristine
its preciousness intact
for all people to share.

Miranda Gibson is the holder of the longest tree-sit record – 449 days in the Styx Valley, Tasmania, 2013.

Goodness

As much as I want to believe in goodness
I can't forget
how people can enter a café,
gun down its diners
like the inconsequential insects
they thought them to be
and walk away, as if nothing happened.

Fears and worries surface
for a cursed planet, a paradise lost.
Those who have power to create change
do nothing.

Innocence has fled
signposts everywhere –
grotesque toddlers
bop along beauty pageant catwalks,
Teenagers roam lonely, littered streets
tattooed, pierced, studded
searching for a tribe to belong to
clutching at mobile phones
a new generation
with different ideals of success, beauty and love.

But what about those who still roam the earth
like the Inuit, Laplander, Roma gypsy?
They own four-wheel drives,
credit cards,
conned into a world of 'things'
before stagnation set in
to seduce and sicken them,
no longer able to travel the old roads.

What happens when the last nomad dies
and no more offerings are made
in tribute to mother earth?
What tribe will any of us belong to?

Can goodness overcome greed and tyranny?
Can Jesus and the Prophet and the Buddha
be acknowledged as the messengers they were,
not the harbingers of war they've become?

I want to believe in goodness for all of us.
I need it like the air we breathe
the sun that warms us
the water we drink.

The beauty of our planet brings me to my knees.

I want to kneel for an eternity
and bask in goodness.
Surely that's not too much to ask?

A Dog's Tale

for Bernard

The little dog, after the family
left Algeria,
was saved by their father
who organised it\s passage
by ship to Marseilles.

Little Vrac* had travelled the desert
with their father, loyal confidant
sitting close, as he drove his truck
sleeping in his tent at night,
kept safe from the other workers
attempting to feed Vrac alcohol
in puerile attempts at amusement.

And so, the faithful companion
found himself with his family
in a new land –
a place of exciting new smells.

One evening in Marseilles
they sat to share a meal,
little Vrac
going to each of them
in turn,
then curling up
at their mother's feet
to die a peaceful death.

Here ends the tale of little Vrac –
of a loving farewell
too sweet to be left untold.

Vrac: French for disorderly, higgledy piggledy

The Itinerant

For years he'd lived in a tent
out bush
making do as best he could.
He'd travelled all over Australia
ending up in Tasmania
haunted by relentless urges
of a manic mind,
a monster needing constant feeding.

He'd experienced many jobs,
the one he loved best
a cook,
but when re-emerging illness struck
he was forced to move on,
a boss unable to cope
with a man who couldn't get to work on time,
who struggled with daily demands
of a society that couldn't shift the usual view.

Sitting in the summer sun
he reads voraciously
a restless mind,
self-taught, intelligent
his occasional rapid bursts of conversation
frenetic,
his depth, perception and compassion
revealed a person with boundless gifts
misunderstood, cast off
no supports in place –
self-medicating, no permanency.

I watched him prepare food
for the people who had given him
a temporary home; clean, meticulous
swift movements from kitchen bench to stove
totally focussed
like a dancer repeating well-known steps

and an ache rose in me
for all his beauty and grace
for those who could not love him
for those who'd turned him away
unaware of the majesties within

Reflections on Budapest

Budapest stirs up a heat in me
an inner division, like the city

Buda from where I stand,
its Castle District, Fishermen's Bastion
luminous in whispering sand-gold stone,
tree-lined dappled pathways
shimmering lime-green in gentle sunlight,
black ravens, sacred bird of Magyars
strutting ancient cobbled paths –
and across the Danube, Pest
two halves becoming one
linked by imposing bridges

This beautiful city sparkles
a cultured, patriotic people –
Hero's Square, the Millennium Monument
Archangel Gabriel atop its central pillar,
and on the stand below, great bronzed statues
Hungary's seven chieftains and their horses
who led the Magyar tribes to settle
in this land,
one thousand years of nationhood,
speakers of a unique language, lending sweetness
to the ear, creating a separateness
from other Europeans –
leaving them strangers when venturing abroad

Elegant long avenues like Andrássy Street,
manicured parklands flushed full with summer flowers,
neoclassical pillars of thermal baths
a haven for well-being,
floating chess games –
a magnificent Gothic Parliament
one of the largest in the world
home to the Holy Crown
symbolic head of a nation
and beneath its head, the venerated body of its people
battles fought, blood shed in freedom's name

The Archangel Gabriel appears everywhere
levitating above city buildings
holding aloft the Holy Crown,
with its double cross of Christianity

Legend says the angel
instructed Pope Sylvester in a dream
to adorn the head of István with this precious crown,
Hungary's first Christian king,
who then declared the Blessed Virgin Mary
mother and protector of his peoples

In all my explorations
my father's birthplace and history
stared back at me,
its many glories and sorrows
shaped by a Magyar spirit
refusing to kneel before invaders
their last courageous uprising in 1956
fighting Soviet tanks with stones and stolen guns

All this I thought, and more
the day I visited my grandparent's graves
laying summer flowers at their headstone
never destined to meet them
too late for me, too late

Years later I discovered
they were exiles here in Budapest
fleeing Erdély in 1920, after Trianon
torn from their ancestral Székely heartland
dying far from home

Budapest stirs up a heat in me
how can I quench this fire?

Erdély: The Magyar name for Transylvania. Transylvania, from the Latin translation of the Hungarian *Erdöelve* meaning 'Beyond the Forest.'
Trianon: In 1920, after World War I, greater Hungary was compelled to sign the Treaty of Trianon. She lost almost three-fourths of her territory and two-thirds of her inhabitants.
Székely: In AD 946, one of the Hungarian tribes settled there as border guards in the easternmost tip of Transylvania. *Szék* meaning chair or seat, well-organised military districts, referring to complete administrative and judicial power vested in their own chiefs. This region is known as Szkélyföld, 'Land of the Székelys', which is now part of Romania. Ethnic Hungarians trapped behind new borders suffer discrimination and economic persecution.

The Bridge at Csikrákos

Erdély (Transylvania)

Carried in my hands, earth from a grave
a small silk parcel, ribbon-bound
an offering from Tasmania
my father's final resting place –
both now together in his ancestral land.

I spoke for him, a promise kept
prayers observed by none but sun and moon
and gazing out at furrowed fields
it seemed that for a moment
distant mountains heard me, leaning forwards
listening in,
'Dad, I've brought you home again.'

Erdély, home of the Széke Magyars
from where all my courage springs
unknown for decades, now understood
it is a living thing.

Beneath green lacing limbs of spreading larch
on a little bridge across the River Olt
hot tears fell, baptised my cheeks and lips
I recall their stinging salt.

High upon the cresting hill
a lonely chapel stood
sole witness to a heartfelt plea
seeking peace and restitution
for a father's wandering exiled soul.

Like a flock of birds, words hovered, taking wing
gliding over sweeping valleys, forests, hills
beneath the bridge, clear water purling by
the tumbling stream Dad knew when young.

He was never a child of Budapest
I did not understand, but now I do
Ah, the beauty of this ancient land
passed on through him –
its preciousness abides in me.

I unwrapped the silken cloth
released the earth and watched it fall
to flow and merge in every tributary –
like blood in veins,
his body mingling with the earth
to find the roots of trees
paddling toes of children's feet
to be drunk by horses, bees and grasses
wolves and birds and butterflies
by all that grows, and is nourished here.

Entreaties rose and fell, in breaths
like life itself
merged with babbling sounds of water
like a baby's mewling cry,
my dispossession torn away
a birthing wound healed up
his history and mine entwined
like flowers upon a spreading vine.

The cross upon the chapel
spread long shadows like a stain –
a faith of generations imbedded here
death, rebirth
forever turning like a wheel
Protectors, Széke Magyars all.

Here I stand
a thousand years have passed
grandparents' villages nearby to me
testament to courage, strength and will
to those safeguarding all in Erdély.

I tied my parcel's ribbon to a tree
a scrap of cloth, to flutter in each season
a parting token left to fade with time –

I sensed a thousand glittering eyes
observe my every move
forebears approaching softly
to dry my tears
to take my hands in theirs
surround me with their love
to welcome me and kiss me, still.

Towards Istanbul

From the little travelling boat
breathtaking views
city walls monumental,
a skyline of mosques, turrets and towers
stupendous in design and colour
domes ballooning up like wind-filled sails
crammed full with the breath of supplications

Five times each day
from needle-pointed minarets
muezzins perfect trilling syllables,
prayers shifting and layering themselves
in skeins and nets of adoration
cast heavenwards

Entreaties to God on High drift everywhere
curling around Topkapi Palace
marble pavilions pressing the Bosphorus
brightly carved ornamental kiosks
tree-filled parklands
Hagia Sophia, Hagia Irene
where holy icons gaze out once more
upon uplifted faces of believers,
a faith of generations subjugated
ancient lamentations embedded in their stone

There are layers within layers here,
undeniable truths
flow through this fairy-tale city
exposing a nakedness,
a sense of all-pervading history
lingering in streets and cobbled alleyways
of swords and blood and war
feuds and festivals
of the beautiful and strong
the cruel and malicious,
memory swirling like veils of fine and precious fabric
now disintegrating with age, fading like a dream

Empires raised and lost,
peoples hunted and haunted
a city whose power, might, wealth and faith
formed schisms between West and East
and left its mark
shaping the turbulent centuries to come

All this and more drifts and sighs,
whispering on dove-green waters of the Marmara Sea

Ah, Istanbul, enchanting temptress
to fend off those darker thoughts
to look with open eyes and innocence
upon your hypnotic splendours
sees all your transgressions disappear

Aghios Nikolaos

Crete

Across Mirabello Bay
the sea spreads cornflower-blue
waves opal-tipped,
mountains rising
like the backs of gods

Within their folds
small villages clung tenuously
like patches of camomile
and as night fell, windows winked –
a host of fireflies dancing in the dark

Aghios Nikolaos layers itself upwards,
busy, winding streets
markets offering fresh produce
trinkets, baubles
blue glass eyes, for protection
silver Cretan priestesses
snakes whirling about their heads

From the curving harbour
a place to sit, enjoy –
boats coming, going
trailing lacy ribbons
sails like white handkerchiefs
fluttering in a village dance

A mother follows her toddler
hands guiding little shoulders,
hums a haunting tune
as if to remind the mountains
they belong here,
men gathered at outdoor tables
heads inclined, deep in conversation
carved wooden doors of an old café
flung open in welcome
tiny red and white tiles patterning the floor

Cretan music enticing from the inner darkness
smells of coffee, raki, tobacco smoke –
holy trinity of men's addictions

The colossal moon at night
ate up the sky
light forging unearthly pathways
on the sea
hypnotic beauty denying sleep
stars like fists of Daphne
flowering on high

On the town's outskirts
the local cemetery's wrought-iron gates
an imposing portal for mourners
treading gently
flower-laden hands,
flickering candles set in red glass
death and life entwined
flames of faith and love
strong here, like the marble headstones
of the men who carved them

The little town poured out
its courtesies and hospitalities,
the young girl from our hotel
face like a Cretan princess
black hair streaming silk in her wake
sped by, on a scooter
waving, smiling, wishing us well
as we walked, arm in arm, a perfect night

Flight over Arabian Peninsula

Looking down from the aircraft
land appears barren
in Arabic, *Rub' al Khali*
The Empty Quarter

Sand, billions of grains
constantly moving, forming different shapes
and to know 'star' dunes exist
conjures up in my mind
a majestic night sky
filled with lustrous stars
a brilliant moon
reflected in those very grains
of glistening sand

Silence and space
shift human consciousness
peoples here birthing new thought
a metamorphosis
for changing mankind's destiny –
worship and belief systems diverse
the veneration of Ra, Astarte
Alilat, Jesus, Mohammed –
all have left their mark

This is not emptiness at all
it is a place of richness
of profound and mystical awakenings

The traveller feels gratitude
for all those
who once walked the deserts far below
teaching us to reach for greater heights
within ourselves

www.ingramcontent.com/pod-product-compliance
Lightning Source LLC
Chambersburg PA
CBHW062154100526
44589CB00014B/1832